CURVED SPACE

SUSAN TERRIS

EDITOR'S CHOICE: NATIONAL POETRY BOOK SERIES 1998
LA JOLLA POETS PRESS

ISBN: 0-931721-15-6
Library Of Congress Number: 97-76567
First Edition

La Jolla

P O E T S   P R E S S

Kathleen Iddings Editor/Publisher

P.O. Box 8638
La Jolla, CA 92038

Cover & Author Photograph:
Diane Rosenblum Althoff
Berkeley, CA

Cover Design:
Patricia R. Barnett
127 Spinnaker Court
Del Mar, CA 92014

ACKNOWLEDGMENTS

Some of the poems in this volume have appeared in various forms in the following magazines and journals:

The Antioch Review: "**Snake**," "**What Margaret Knew**"
Barnabe Mountain Review: "**Spider**"
Billee Murray Denny Poems 1995-96: "**Elegy For The Family** "
The Birmingham Review: "**Boundary Waters**"
Black Mountain Review: "**Lena Grove**," "**Scarlett**"
Blue Unicorn: "**Tess**," "**Dark Of The Moon**"
Calyx: "**Washrag**"
The Comstock Review: "** Season Of Burnt Offerings**"
The Creative Woman: "**Yelena**"
Descant: "Yelena's Kiss"
Gaia: "**Dark Of The Moon**"
The Galley Sail Review: "**The Man Who Stood On A Chair**"
Iowa Woman: "**Molly Has The Last Word**"
In Vivo: "**False Pregnancy**"
Iris: "**Mermaids**"
Kansas Quarterly: "**Hel**," "**Irene's Saga**"
Negative Capability: "**Wide Spectrum**"
Nimrod: "**Heading North**"
Pig Iron: "Madrone"
Plainsongs: "**Onions**"
Poet & Critic: "**Flesh**"
Poet Lore: "**Self-Sufficiency**," "**False Pregnancy**"
Poetpourri: "**Summer Solstice**," "**On Black Sunday**"
Poetry Northwest: "**Hester's Grammar**" as "**A Lesson In Tense**"
Poetry Now: "**Anna**" as "**That Woman**," "**Emma's Flat**"
     as "**The Apartment**"
Poets On: "**Hester's Grammar**"
Painted Bride Quarterly: "**The Sound Of Your Mother Chewing**"
Primavera: "**Guinevere**" as "**Baited**"
Rattle: "**Onions**"
Sheila-Na-Gig: "**Mourning Cloak**," "**Bones**"
Southern California Anthology: "**Elegy For The Family**"
The Sow's Ear Poetry Review: "**Forgiveness**"
The Spoon River Poetry Review: "**Flossie**," First Memory,"
     "**Green Shade**"
South Coast Poetry Journal: "**Luck**"
Southern Humanities Review: "**Palatino**"
Southern Poetry Review: "**The Wringer**"
Staple: "**Ophelia**" as "**Green Girl**"
13th Moon: "**The Thread**"
Wisconsin Review: "**Quiz Kid**"
Worcester Review: "**Lena Grove**"

Poems from this volume have received prizes in the following competitions:

"Elegy For the Family" — Ann Stanford Competition,
  Southern California Anthology 1995
  Billee Murray Denny Competition 1995
"Molly Has The Last Word" — *Iowa Woman* 1995
"Winter Solstice" — Anna Davidson Rosenberg
  Competition for Poems on the Jewish Experience, 1994

Poems from this volume have appeared in the following anthologies:

Anthology of Magazine Verse & Yearbook of American
Poetry 1997: "Self-Sufficiency"
Claiming The Spirit Within: 1996, Beacon Press,
  "Forgiveness"
Hot Flashes: Faber & Faber, 1995, "Flesh"
Nice Jewish Girls: Penguin Books, 1996, "Winter Solstice
  " as "Baba"
Topics For Getting in Touch: Pudding House Publications,
  1996, "The Thread"
Words & Quilts: Quilt Digest Press, 1994, "Forgiveness"

Some poems from this volume were published in a chapbook: Killing In The Comfort Zone: Pudding House Publications, 1995.

The quote from "Elegy" by David St. John is from Study For The World's Body and is reprinted by permission of the author and of HarperCollins.

The four African terms and definitions used in "Elegy For The Family" are from John Julius' book Cracker.

For my family... with much love

TABLE OF CONTENTS

I. INHALING STARS

II. OUT-OF-BODY

III. BRIGHT AND DUSKY TONES

Sometimes the drawers of the earth close;
Sometimes our stories keep on and on. So listen---

— Elegy, David St. John

INHALING STARS

First Memory

There was a dripping spigot and another girl,
her name the same as mine.
Her Dutched hair, size, and smocked dress
mimicked me, too.
But I held no Dy-Dee doll with
cherub mouth, whose red-nippled bottle
tasted like gum, smelled like tricycle tires;
so with stealth I stalked that Doppelgänger.
Patient even then, waiting until our mothers,
voices braided into impenetrable strands,
receded I struck.
Swift and vicious, I prized the bottle from that girl,
shattered it on the pavement.
As she wailed, I — anxious to possess
beauty — scooped up fistfuls of new-made diamonds,
unconcerned by needles of pain
or bright leakage between my fingers.

SAN MARINO

During an early visit to that island —
a Rousseau-leafed Eden where ribbons
of light banded doors, ice cubes
rattled, and gardenia-scent
greased the patio, oozed the air —
I met death. *After the first death...*

Barefoot and inattentive, I pulped
a lizard on the walk. Then, cleaning
my foot on grass short and hard
like golf greens, I sidled off to watch
Churchill whose cigar aped brush
thrusts as he colored Biscayne Bay.

Later, my shoulders sun-lashed, afire,
observing Grandmother's jade,
Poppa's racetrack squint, I palmed Poppa's
twenty-dollar bill, shivered the finger bowl,
mourning yet unable to say why
I had no autograph. *...there is no other.*

ONIONS

Potatoes would grow behind my ears,
they said, if I didn't wash
and radishes beneath my fingernails,
onions beneath arms, corn between toes,
carrots amid the sheep's-path of my part.
Watermelon vines and apple trees would
flourish within from seeds
swallowed as I ate too fast,
careless of details as I was with
all aspects of a fragile, corporeal self.
Inside my nose or navel,
between my legs were other unclean places
no one mentioned, freeing me to suspect
leeks, chives, parsley, wild mustard,
as I probed with curious fingers, tasted.

A sly, secretive child dedicated to sowing
seeds of sedition, I reveled that
my alien, vinegar-onion-sweat-scented
green-brown body could contain seeds.
Woody, potato-eyed, sporting tubers,
fronds, vines, stalks, blossoms over
layer within translucent layer, I raced.
And then, tying sashes of smocked dresses
high to simulate pregnancy,
I marched in measured cadences,
convinced that fruit and vegetable pips
cached now in my womb and at other sites
would someday germinate to produce
round — if still unclean and reeking — creatures:
strange-bright mirror-image selves.

SELF-SUFFICIENCY

"Breathe in experience, breathe out poetry."
— *Poem Out Of Childhood*, Muriel Rukeyser

The cave of her room was where she practiced,
unrolling grass mat and red-draping
lampshade to simulate firelight.
Hand prints muraled walls behind bookcases.
Silkworms in jars scalloped mulberry leaves
while she awaited cocoons whose fiber would
unwind and spin garments to clothe her.
On the bulb atop the lamp, dime-sized biscuits
and birds' eggs sizzled.
To maintain strength, she prowled the room's
perimeter from bookcase to bed
to dresser to chair to radiator to windowsill,
careful not to let her feet brush ground.

Moments of rest, by candlestub-light,
she kept Angrian journals in left-handed code,
illustrated with nymphets
whose hairless bodies mirrored her own.
Her deities that cycle were storybook dolls
by Nancy Ann. Pouffed in satin and tulle,
they pursed bee-sting lips, gazed from alcoves
while she, shadow matter, waited for bisque arms
to lift mouse-paw hands in benediction,
a sign she might shrug her cocoon
and with pale silk-moths fly out,
taste a world where
black-veined monarchs shiver the air.

THE WRINGER

Flattened yet joined, they mingle
and embrace with abandon.
Impressions of buttons tattoo chests
when father-sister-brother arms
intertwine as mother slowly feeds
the wringer. She's silent under
bare yellow bulbs, frown
stapling an 11 between her eyes.
I, forbidden to turn the handle,
watch and recall odd asides about
tits caught in wringers. At ten, I have
no tits but feel a wet-thrill
when male sleeves and pantlegs
elbow or knee my soft cotton dresses.
Sometimes anticipating this, I lie
encaged beneath the chute inhaling
sweat, memorizing masculinity of
unclean clothes before washer
and wringer moist-fuse them. Inside,
tangled garments are mother's

but outside, they're mine. Sensuously,
I peel them apart and drape them cuff
to cuff along fraying white lines.
Wooden pins like faceless soldiers
secure contact but see nothing.
As wind frenzies limbs to
dances of damp rapture, I dart
barefoot among them, my shadow

coupling with shirts, open-fly pajamas.
The whip-snap of cloth in sunshine
quickens me. Hip pressed to hip,
I glide a forbidden tango with father,
with brother, with men I've yet to meet.
Hidden from mother, I sway with
erotic ecstasy, grow tits and body hair,
I bleed, open myself to future sin,
to days of carnal lust
and the sweetness of earthly delights.

DARK OF THE MOON

In the garden, girl in a white gown
barefoots among fireflies and night-moths.
Under crooks of Douglas fir, she hears
an owl ruff his feathers and mourning doves
refold their wings.

The earth is cooling, shrinking, drying.
Rotted tomatoes, red-black sacs, droop
from stems. A pumpkin yellows
on its spined umbilical, and marigold dust
warps skin inside her nose.

Strung tree to tree, paper lanterns
ghost the air.
As she stretches toward their warmth,
shadows stir, chords shiver her ears.
Apparitions vapor from
the soil and wind around her.
She reaches out. *Dance,*
she commands them, *you must dance.*

Responsive, they sheer toward music
and lantern light. She watches
them beckon. Then she joins in, eager
to mimic their ease. Feet skip over dirt,
leaf, stone. Her enchanters

are shape and flame yet faceless.
Bats flare above her head. A possum
scrabbles claws on bark. Though she is

flushed, shades are pale.
White grays, and she sees through
their cornstalk bones. To keep them close,
she cries, *Sing, you must sing,*
yet even as her voice rises,
music thins to threads. An echo

of melody and image lap, fusing
now and soon. Shades retreat,
lanterns dim until she is left alone
where night is onyx cold,
and nothing quickens below the fir.

Her legs are shrouded by her gown.
Breast buds tender, joints and sinews liquid.
Footprints craze mud beneath her feet.
To ward off chill, she reaches out,
lets a firefly pink the soft cup of her hands.

THE THREAD

This is not the first time
I have written about the blue skirts.

Something about them trails
a thread I can't seem to cut.
So let's begin again at the beginning.
Together, my two friends and I chose
sky-blue cotton and white eyelet,
sewed bottom-ruffled garments.
But then, before the school pageant,
I treadled Baba's ancient Singer
to create a pink-striped batiste
and another for my tiny sister.
In the pageant, I appeared not with
Rosalind and Eleanor as primaveras,
garlanded virgins dancing on the grass,
but as a Byzantine madonna angling
a shadow over my child.
I had felt compromised when
confronted with forming an arc
of an innocent trio; yet as madonna
I was not alone but still unique,

compelling. I'd found my role.
Spin. Measure. Clip.

LUCK

Gnomes curdled the milk, and butter wouldn't churn.
She sensed disaster, as in Dickens
when clocks stop to mark the hour of death.

She eyed her drawer, peering past lop-eared rabbit
and spun-glass goose, behind barrettes
and old keys, at her stash — *I've got tuppence...*
nickels, pennies, quarters, francs, kroner,
shillings — coins dropped on paths waiting for

... jolly, jolly tuppence ... her claim.
This providential money was to be saved forever
(like knee-scabs she'd kept as a child),
testament to health and fortune — dowry ...
to last me all my life... to be buried with her:
a promise of good purchase in the afterworld.

When her husband acknowledged four quarters
he'd borrowed then replaced with impostors,
his apologies were dross. Butter still wouldn't churn.
Clocks were stopped. Luck ran through her fingers.
A scab lost in the river had ruined one collection,

and he'd ruined another. But, as she flung coins
from the bureau, she saw she possessed a doorkey
to every place she'd lived.
Then her sweet butter began to set.

SEA-BABY

The baby cannot be real.

Shell of an ear, starfish hand
and tide-smell of infant, still, she is
weightless on my breast, chalky,
mouth open, hair like bleached kelp,
arms with no elbows reaching out.

Once she rocked in water.

As I was wading, careful to avoid
rosettes of coral, I found her supine
in a pool, a sea-baby, stiff arms drying
like driftwood; so I knelt,
netted her, cradled her and sang.

The baby cannot be real,

I tell my husband, drawing him
from dreams as the child begins
to tinge yellow, stipple, gill, fold in
on herself. *She's too small to keep,*
he mumbles, tugging at the net.

Once she rocked in water,

but now, arms caught and severing
from the body, she's trapped, and
I'm crying. *Don't,* my husband says,
nuzzling as we sink.
Remember the arms of the sea star.

SNAKE

As inflamed voices grate,
the child pivots toward the wall,
thumb in mouth,
and eyes the Merlin puppet
suspended from the cabinet knob.
Her other hand, pocketed, writhes
in cotton gauze until her dress dips drunkenly
to baste the cuffs of multi-striped socks,
rouse hints of fresh peach
from a melting body. Her mother
is weeping now, expelling faint, feral gasps.
But the child does not turn her head. Instead,
uncorking the sour-smelling thumb, she crooks
the cord dandled from Merlin's robe and
tugs. "Watch out," she says
in a sugar-tit, once-upon-a-time tone,
addressing both thumb
and wall. "The man has a wild snake
hiding behind his dress."

ON BLACK SUNDAY

Ice encrusts willow branches, and the wind
clicks them like teeth. Deaf to that chatter,
dreaming of wheels and wind, my husband
browses catalogues as our daughter,
crooning off-key, frosting lips, conjures
lovers to carpet her away.

My husband, my daughter are unsuspecting.
While I cast a barbed but barren lure, they
prepare to fork flesh from the bone.
As I tromp on unfermented fruit, they sniff fumes
of cabernet, ignoring the Bible's maxim
on sowing and reaping.

Untainted by Sunday's bleakness, those two
are unaware I taste ashes on my tongue,
smell rotted eggs, feel eyes film.
Squinting, I see engines collide, anthracite
crack, tornadoes suck, blood congeal
the pelts of baby seals.

While I flay my arms to deflect blackness,
they breathe myths. Unaware of the tiger
chuffing, they reel in a glade of ginger,
float at the crest of a wave.
As I shiver, they rise on waxen wings
oblivious to the arc of the sun.

HEL

In Teutonic myth, a mortal must have
a saga to enter Valhalla,
so she's left her featherbed birth kingdom,
turned nomad to create her saga.

Anarchist, road warrior,
urban Indian creeping from squat
to squat moving west, she lives
in groups yet is alone. Hair is spiked,
ears, nose, lips pierced. Clothes are
oiled to her skin. She dopes, drinks,
panhandles: a ptomaine queen, with crown
of flies, dumpster-diving for survival.

When she has felt pens or paint, she writes
her saga on public walls. *Escape pain.*
All is flux: nothing stays still.
Commit random deeds of kindness and senseless
acts of beauty.
Or she poses questions with enigmatic replies.
Who am I? A weed on a burning plain.
Where am I going? Ragna rök: a fatal destiny.

Once, as a fur-swaddled child, she teethed on
mythologies,
ingesting Hel, daughter of Loki,
sister of the wolf Fenrir and serpent Midgard,
whose head hung forward and who had
a face half-human and half-blank.

Now, after shucking the winter-pale ermine
that failed to warm, she is Hel.
Days, she calls herself by that name.
Nights, shrouded in green-black plastic, she stays
awake to contemplate Valhalla
and its elusive nature. Jousting with sleep,
she tries to fend off dreams.
Dreams are lies. Dreams are truth.
Ragna rök. She does not dare to dream.

GREEN SHADE

Kneeling alone in a chill orchard, you shake branches
and gather windfall. Beware — *a green thought
in a green shade* — of what you wish for.
In the tentative way women are conditioned
to ask for the things they want, you wished for
a daughter; and, yes, she seemed
perfect; so how could you suspect
olive eyes, pale skin, tufts of tangled hair?

You sent her along wild paths, offered the chase,
rush of blood sport. Later, she sank milk-fangs
in your throat and began to drink. Had you
seen signs, understood ungovernable impulses,
menace under soft flesh, you might have
strung garlic cloves about your neck
or sought a midnight crossroad to drive a stake
through her heart. *Too cruel*, you say,
much too cruel? Bone of your bones, flesh of your flesh:
instead, you've let her suck you dry.
Now while you succumb, she grows,

scorning the weakness which nourishes her.
This victory is Pyrrhic; for today — near-orphan —
she wails of abuse and abandonment. Mothers, daughters.
Daughters, mothers. You know you must warn others,
teach them to sniff out rot
below girls' sweet apple-cheeks; but, green shade,
you kneel waiting for blood
to pool and let down so she can, once more, latch on.

BOUNDARY WATERS

I was guiding a trip where a young boy drowned.
Near Ely, he knifed into yellow-green,
stroked past humped boulders and never came up.

Then a second boy donned goggles and angled
himself deep where schools of dark fish finned.
I watched, held my breath, waited,

saying, *This is taking too long.* Goggles bobbed up,
but not his head, and he was lost to me, also.
I told myself, *This is not true, only a dream,*

and so I undrowned him, summoned him back to
balance on gunwales, a delicate, sinewy form,
skin stretched taut over ribcage. As I watched,

he dove and swam, rising again and again from
a bottomless lake. Then I summoned the first boy
until, water dribbling from hair and shoulders,

he stood before me, gave me a zippered pouch.
In it, crimped bills and fragments of cold
rock crystal. Turning away from boundary waters,

I mounted a horse, pulled one boy to the saddle
behind me, then the other. Wind and grit
in teeth, I loped through forests of jack pine

feeling water sucked from my clothing. The boys
dried, too, growing lighter until they, like birch bark,
peeled and peeled and flaked away to nothing.

BRITTLE COVENANT

Under chalk-streaked sky, amid robins
gorging pyracantha, I — mourning
lost buds — deadhead roses, discarding
petals soft as newborns' flesh.

Soon reverie yields to moans as I
see not rose or child but
a vagrant ragpile of degradation
deaf to shriek of drunken birds.

"Violation," I gasp, eyeing
this threat splayed in
my garden. *We must keep faith*
with those who lie in the dust.

Faith? Yes, bud, infant, each a marker.
How we begin and end: frail with
blanched, papery husks
tight-fused, involuntary shuddering.

Still, snake in my Eden where I hold only
clippers, I condemn him and myself.
If I held a sword, I might
plunge it, for I know I cannot keep faith.

HEADING NORTH

*There's something about north... something that sets it
apart from all other directions."* — E. B. White

Sunlight lemons the morning, and back
at Mother's under the Thiebaud oil,
I am passive, so when she suggests

lamb chops for dinner with my brother,
I nod, fail to mention I no longer eat meat.

After my tonsils came out, she removed
the bright balloons tied to the bed before I
could inhale their gas, talk like Donald,

fly away. Thus, my maiden scheme for
heading north was thwarted before it began.

But it was one of many: ask at Mary Institute.
Still, when I walk the halls there eyeing
my name engraved in brass, I'm possessed

by a yearning to be May Queen, to wear
a white gown and reenact Mother's life.

Thiebaud says his childhood was happy,
that painting is joy, yet he feels anguish
trapped deep in brightness. To my eyes

his vivid canvases (Who says a sunny
childhood stems dark currents?) point north.

My brother is six-foot-two; yet when we
tangle, he weakens, lets me exercise
primogeniture and chase him to his room

where he has stayed, seldom breaking out
to examine enigmas of degree or direction.

Mind sunburnt, exhaling lemony light,
I again twitch myself from Mother's south,
Brother's south, and I turn north.

SUMMER SOLSTICE

Tree frogs bell the night and black-leafed maple
arabesques against the sky as I, sleepwalking,
Braille through the old house.
Eleven again, I touch parents who lie spooned
in the corner bedroom while elsewhere
a cradled baby thumbs-sucks as her brother,
dog-sweaty, spread-eagles
under Nana's tumbling-block quilt.

Sweet, so sweet I, denying demons, seek the attic.
There past trunks and boxes, Nana's
handsewn wedding dress, yellowed and frail,
shrugs off mauve tissue. Tentative, I
hold out my hands, shimmy it over shoulders
until it satins hips and bare feet.
From the eaves, wind soughs calling up
lost violets and asking: *Why? Where?*
Fingering the violets petal by petal —

loves me, loves me not — I waltz, slowly
at first in a mid-summer's night dream,
then faster until skylights shatter and the gown
begins to deconstruct. Soon, seed pearl
constellations spin above my head, as bobbins
of ecru lace rise and warp the sky.
I try to tame my steps but am possessed by
shades of that garment I loved and lost,
lost with night-safe parents and children,

lost when the old house was sold,
so lost I cannot halt this dance.
Raw boards shred my soles.
Then pain radiates upwards as flesh peels
from my spiraling frame, scales, thins,
flays outward — cool, cooler, cold
down to bones — bare manic bones.

LIFE BYTES

1. Girl

When she fell through ice on the pond, she said
it was an accident, but she did it on purpose,
denying chill or fear, so she could walk on water.

When she climbed out the window, scrabbled
over loose clay tiles, she told herself it was
safe to spring from the roof because she could fly.

When she night-prowled through the old sawmill,
she believed herself invisible, strong enough to
walk through walls, tall enough to touch the moon.

And when she paddled the Flambeau, needled canoes
down through its high, unrunnable rapids,
she knew she'd survive because she was immortal.

2. Woman

When he said he loved her and would do so forever,
she said yes, because she walked through walls
and on water. Then, taking flight, she hung the moon.

Now when the moon waxes and wanes, she ponders
old wounds and fresh crime, aware magic ebbs,
trails grow faint until he is distant and hard to track.

When winter tides rise and fall, when lifelines
fray, she is slurried in and out of undertow
conscious of mortality for he is too deep to reach.

And when blackness rages him, she seeks a lost girl,
a girl who had supernatural powers, because
it is murky and she cannot touch him or the moon.

AUTOMATIC WRITING

In the waxy, flickering darkness,
wheels of the heart-shaped planchette roll
from side to side, up and down,
over and back, responding to the edgy pressure
of their four hands. Grease pencil
in its brass holder marks butcher paper
with fluid, gyroscopic script.

Once four hands gathered wild berries,
bathed hair and feet for one another
in a snow-melt cascade. Once at night on
black pond-ice, four hands spun votive candles,
turned them to winter fireflies. And once
they lay till morning on the hen house roof,
hands warm inside clothes
as Perseid meteors confettied the sky.

Now hands guide the planchette, and tension
rises. *This is bullshit,* he says. *I'm leaving.*
And so it is. And so he does. And when
she examines the butcher paper,
she finds only chicken scratchings
or fragments of a hieroglyphic lament.

CAMERA OBSCURA

She waits in darkness staring down
at the parabola of wave, sand, gull, and rock.
Views shift clockwise and clockwise, breakers siphon
off the curved lip, until the world
is upside-down yet circling to re-right itself.
A pelican skids, beaks a fish, wings over the rim
of the silken bowl. A thin woman dressed
in black, who might be herself, descends stairs
and vanishes in the Musée Mechanique.

Leonardo knew this camera. Vermeer used it
for portraits: a spinning mirror
and lenses — one convex, one concave.
As light glints through an aperture,
a picture roils upon a curve in a dim room.
Standing there watching her spouse and children
rotate out of sight on the beach below,
she feels herself begin to invert
and slide off the surface into nothingness

or coexistence. Leaving the camera, she climbs
to the street and a car hits her. Standing at the curb,
she sees a car hit someone else.
She steps in front of a car and no impact jars.
But maybe she never moved at all. Music, odd and
cymbal-like, dins her head. Moments peel off: history
of what happens or what might be. Perhaps she
can choose memory. Elect the outcome,
dismiss the accident, moment of rape or desertion.

Her children, robust and long-limbed, cavort
yet orbit off the smooth edges
of the arc. Each rotation they are changed,
color-leached, flatter, more distant.
Her husband riffles pages of his paper yet stares
outward toward the breaker line where a windsurfer
luffs a waxy sail. This man with newspaper
is a white-haired stranger in polar fleece.
She might abandon the dark room and meet him
on the beach. She might, like the woman in black,
glide into the Musée, face Laughing Sal's
day-glo ringlets and lewd-jiggle cantaloupe breasts.
Or she may risk the path of the oncoming car,
cross the street and dissolve,
leaving everything and everyone
capsized in the oceanic curve of time.

MADRONE

Some days, I think I'll walk out the door,
never look back, because there's danger
here, quicksand threatening. At night, stud, joist, I-beam, lost luster
creak with menace protesting rusting U-joints,
overloaded circuits, shredded dreams.
If — stifling the healer-voice who intones,
First do no harm — I left, I'd escape mildew,
rot, and other indignities.
A sinkhole, my father called our old house.

While I sleep, the ooze takes all things plumb
and distorts. Still, I've stayed, struggling
against harm when the children roamed yet
trailed stones to pick their way back and din
my solitude, or my spouse — *hok a tchynik* —
assigned me to plumb for him. White nights,
inching barefoot, I'm waylaid. As the sludge
sucks, it groans. Wily, I bargain with it
and the creatures who lurk within.
I promise to stay, hinting offerings and
a small tabernacle if they will grant me time.

Five people, a family like ours, keep house
in my drawer, worry dolls to sleep away care,
yet I invoke other night-talismans
that appear in sets of five — us posed at
Point Lobos, alop on monkey bars
in Alta Park, by a pier in Minnesota, a dory on

the Colorado — bright-hued, with assorted
hair lengths, shoes, sizes next to one another.
But the photograph that rivets suggests us
amid branches of the largest madrone on
Tamalpais. Time has faded our five
to shadows holding hands. Leaves envelop

all, and we, now part of the tree, are ringed
together. On the mountain, near Bon Tempe,
that madrone — cool, aromatic — still sheds bark,
growing ever larger. If I searched I'd find it.
But I won't. It's there as are we, dimmed
to leaf-green haloes with Cheshire smiles.
So, I stay — *First do no harm* — in the sinkhole,
doctoring, offering succor,
because the photograph ghosts me at night
whispering we, although imperfect
and out-of-plumb like the house,
exist: still a circle, a fairy ring, endangered,
yet poised above darkness, above ooze.

GREEN FLASH

A broken sun flattens at the treeline.
Iridescent blue scribbles a path to it,
and small blue suns like clustered grapes
dot the surface of the lake.
Everything stops. The children. Their children.
Color peaches the water, and beauty
seeps into pores. To still the agitation of
day, I drink the light.
When I open my mouth, bubbles of brightness
rise like daytime fireflies. Stripping bare,
I bathe in light, stir concentric circles of gold.
Admitting no shame, I spoon it over hair and
head, nudge it with breasts, belly,
roll in it, then shrug it around my shoulders.

Odd that I can touch the cooling sun but not you.
As fingertips pinch its last paring of light,
I lift my eyes, catch you on the rising moon,
eased past Sea of Crisis toward Ocean of Storms.
Turning away, I mourn the vanished
light and wonder if
the green flash always comes too late.

ELEGY FOR THE FAMILY

1. *Hatinafsi* (Swahili): Used of a person taking an action
   without consulting anyone because he thinks they may
   persuade him not to do it.

Insensible, we turn away as they, family
and others, insist the cloud resembles
a wolf when we see flocked lambs.
Lambs, wolves — there is no
peaceable kingdom where we may lie
together, so action follows:
elopement or wedding to deflect
voices, blot them to odd syllables.
For distance from opposition, we flee
then sing in a key only animals
or unborn children can hear. We sing of
Eden's steeped leaves and sunsets,
figs and peaches and apples, of offspring
we'll lift upon our shoulders,
so they may have views to us unknown.
Hatinafsi, the hordes say as we see lambs.

2. *Baccedha* (Marathi): The bother, fuss, and vexation
   attendant upon the bringing up of children.

Children know more. Dreams sponge minds
as they do, pitting wills against ours.
Sleep-walking begins early, continues.
Mysteries abound. Cause and effect suspend.

Sly, they sever the lines by which we bind
them: arteries, veins, capillaries thrumming

within skins of risk. Then they bruise like ripe
fruit and bruise us, too, but they heal faster.

Children know more. While we would mold
them, they count our crimes, sit in judgment.
Since quickening, they have controlled
our pulses, meted out arrhythmia or measured

beats as they — our curse, our blessing —
flash lustrous rows of pearl to nip us into line.

3. _Avlyachi mot_ (Marathi): A very loose and patched-up
   union based on no consolidation of interests and with
   an ever-present tendency to separation.

We live in the same houses yet beat fists
on different walls, eat in common
yet sleep alone because night draws us apart.
Grown children forget what they knew.
Separateness overrides linked faces, hands.
No x-ray would show us joined breast-to-breast.
After _Mama_ or _Dada_, there is _Mine_.
Where I end, you begin: forces in conflict.
Shared pain or joy is
illusion, since under all is that chant
of _Mine. Mine. Mine._
So how, while spinning
ever-outward, do we hold together?

4. _Akshauhiaf_ (Sinhalese): An army consisting of
21,870 elephants, 21,870 chariots, 65,610 horses,
and 109,350 foot soldiers.

Someone is always counting. Someone
hefting fewer spoils feels diminished.
Troops amass, patrols advance
across borders, shed blood in no-man,
no-woman's land. Flesh and bone
are offered up. Violence
and separateness, though despised, are
fated. Marry, bear children,
strain to keep the hordes from enmity:
a losing battle,

                yet we engage. But why?
Mine. Still, so much darkness,
we, unfocused lambs, dart both to and
from shelter. Husband, wife, children,
children's children — we chant _mine_, but this
is a wind-song. Even as we amass
matériel to make us impregnable,
the losses begin,
littering the ground as sunrise
rewarms our unpeaceable continuum.

OUT-OF-BODY

DAME ALYS

...Bath

He gave it to me rosy-round,
flesh firm to the touch.

Morning: birdsong trebles the air
as I rise and dance the whited orchard,
buoyed by hidden tunes
and by sweep of journey still ahead.

When I sampled sugar-tart meat,
juice dribbled from my chin
toward crevices of clavicle.

Mid-day: I hold an apple in my palm
and loll in the shade
of a honey locust as its blossom lips
whisper of untasted joy.

Teeth and bone. Apple, too,
ever since Eve, forbidden;
yet I devoured every morsel.

Night: a last bright exclamation
marks the west, and I watch a dragonfly
above fiddleheads. Out of time,
the dragonfly tells me, out of season,

And what did I leave? The mottled core,
a core and two dark pips....

warning, like edges of an old map:
Beware. Here there be dragons.

47

PENELOPE

... Ithaca

Gossamer
like the weaving
of a spider's web. No promises.
Nothing but sheen
in sunlight.

Wind, seas, and siren songs may keep
you, but I breathe asphodel,
loom the day, unravel the night.
You know currents
and cormorant cry, but I know
hearth-heat.

Carpe diem,
say the Romans as spiders
skein. *Gaudeamus igitur,* they advise
in blithe tones as flies
skim toward spittled strands.
Break the web if you will.
It's only meant to remind — *words
like winter snowflakes —*
how gossamer are the threads
spun from one to one.

Yes, I love, though I'd rather
spin stories than lie beneath
an airless shadow.
Too removed to know my freedom?
Sad. A want of imagination.

GUINEVERE

...Camelot

Bread crumbs stipple the face
of an oily black pond on
a night when frogs
have gobbled up the moon.

Crouched in the shallows
shadowed by a regiment
of cattails, she watches
both her lover and her mate.

Their crumbs, water-plumped,
fan lace-like over lily pads
tantalizing,
as she, encircled,

struggles to remember how
it was when she had
no webbing stretched beneath
arms or splayed between toes.

BERTHA MASON'S SONNET

...Thornfield Hall

Flames seep yellowed blood across the heath.
Back-lit, a water-marked silhouette floats,
is consumed. Eerie to feel nostrils pinched
by reek, yet be too numbed to know
its menace. A cricket, cymballing legs, sings
in the glade. For sanctuary, I, too, sing.
As fire plumes, it purifies, creating
refuge where sheep may safely graze.
Anxious to drown madding cries,
I lullaby the night, ask absolution.
Muffled sanity is all I seek. But lured by
embers, swallowed then
released, I phoenix from the ashes
aware rapture, like pain, is seldom earned.

TESS

...Vale of Blackmoor

Any country girl should
grasp the difference between hay and straw,
between provisions and residue. "Waste not,
want not," my simple mother often said.
"And remember the golden rule..."
Yet she failed to speak of alchemy or fate.

One Mayday as straw flecked beneath my feet,
I, beribboned, danced
following an elusive skein,
a reeling cat's-eye taw,
until, slippers shredded, I heard bells chiming
while roosters gloated past the sunrise.
Then hidden by a bough,
languishing on hay, I endeavored to spin
gold. I persisted until,
disheartened,
I tendered chicory to the hens.

Soon the ailing hens refused to lay,
and my father whispered, "Damaged goods."
Later, he sighed, "Straw. Straw...."

OPHELIA

...Elsinore

She woke to a mocking bird and sensed a lucky day.
Face decaled against panes, she browsed
the morning. Unjacketed, she flung herself past
blue door and gate, skinked across the grass
to where he lay, coiled, waiting.
Unsifted, she offered rosemary, pansies. Unsifted,
she exulted when hair tangled to silken knots and
stockings pleated at her ankles. *I love you,* she
breathed, then breathed it again, thirsty for
his reply. But as he rolled her
in grass cuttings, she felt tiny sharpened spears
prick, draining away green, fading all to brown.

YELENA

...Estate Serebriakoff

Bored, I tell you, fanning myself, pacing
languidly amid shades of blue — carpet,
drapery, spirits. But what I think of
is my work, ligatures about your neck

losing slack. Not the water nymph
I seem but a murderous Circe, in me
the dispassionate hides the possessed.
All assassins have monograms. Mine

is slow torture — grass-snake summers
where wild lupine stalks hillsides
as I fancying sisal, tape, wire, hemp,
confess only to boredom. Passion flickers,

possibilities evolve. But I shut my eyes,
because I kill in the comfort zone —
blue waters, blue veins,
an eternity of blue-black cyanosis.

Endgame. The boneyard. For you and me:
no angels nor sky sparked with diamonds.

HESTER'S GRAMMAR

...Boston

I lay my skirt across a chair and it lies there.
   (Present.)
I laid my slippers on the floor and they lay there.
   (Past.)
I have laid myself upon a quilt and I have lain there.
   (Perfect.)

He lays his pants by my skirt and they lie there.
   (Present.)
He laid his boots beside my slippers and they lay there.
   (Past.)
He has laid his body next to mine and it has lain there.
   (Perfect.)

Lay, lies,
laid, lay
laid, lain.
All quite grammatically correct and, still, it is not
the lay or laid that bothers him but the lies.

He may love to lie with me, yet to lie about me is for him
a tense not coped with in any text of standard usage.
   (Imperfect.)

EMMA

...Yonville L'Abbaye

The place we use has public stairs
where red-swirled carpet flaunts
lost knots of hair while coughing up
the smell of Tuesday's cabbage.

In my dreams, when we lie together,
our place is green and slick as pond ice,
and Mother, forgetful of my husband,
appears greeting us benignly.

Other guests wander by. Mother serves
canapés. Guests eat. They drink.
Their smiles illuminate dark corners.
And as we touch, they observe.

But soon the frozen algae softens
from our warmth, thawing the dream place
until it begins to threaten
wisps of hair, whiffs of cabbage.

DAISY'S DREAM

...East Egg

To fringes of the morning, I'll ride with you
and to the cape of light beyond.
Your nickering, your flared nostrils signal,
but I am drawn by rein of brow.

Faces of druids rust up from granite
nodding. Fingers of iceplant, red by day,
lurid by night, point as dune grass whips
shins when I — stumbling across rough ground —
run to catch you. As a girl, I never
gripped horseflesh between my thighs,
because I thought water was all. Salt taste
on my tongue, I faced Goose-Eye,
the unrunnable rapid, choose the wave's edge,
paddled, swam it, survived being thrown
loose from gravity.
Yes, I bled and scarred, but scar tissue
is stronger than other skin.

Now your eye, like Goose-Eye, fills with
turbulence, washing over, wringing out air.
I gasp. You bend until I reach out.
Then looking up toward pale moon mares,
I ride beneath the surf, inhaling
mysteries — dark and light.
Maybe only once. Maybe never again.
As your tail furls and unfurls,
I hold for life, oh my moon horse,
my sea horse, yet never mine at all except
for a brief cycle of chase and of song.

IRENE'S SAGA

...Montpellier Square

He called. They met for lunch.
Talk drifted, except when he noted
she still taunted by thrusting

breasts above the table. Then he,
riffling clouds, suggested postprandials
at a quiet inn. Another jest,
she thought; yet as he etched her
cheek with a kiss, she knew he'd call

again. He did, provocative when
he appeared in her room in women's wear:
a wig, navy suit, and high-heeled boots.
Before she could speak, he, ignoring
the maid who looked on, collared her,
kissed her. She tasted tobacco
and felt, beneath his pegged skirt,
tumescence. Reeling, they landed on

the downstairs hearth where he, still
in woman's garb, informed her spouse
and guests he was her mother,
mother to a child who gave no heart-ache.
Then he crooked an arm across
her chest. *You are good*, he said, pressing
against her, *a good child. Call on me.*

So she called. *Last night*, she said, *I dreamed of you.*
I know, he answered. *The high heels hurt my feet.*

UNDINE

...Lusitania

After the leaving, the long, dry loving.
All that has ended was obsession,
so parting was more logic than sea-change.
Once danger was palpable,
the dream where our children writhed
in forked branches of coral
became too real.
Now, without rake of lashes, we spin
out impersonal lines,
weaving strands of our children.
The net we create is for safety
lest we dip again into pools of madness.

After me, he says with quiet sanity,
there has never been another.
Since we've been apart, volcanic ash
has altered colors of the sunset
and milky, eyeless fish have found their way
to new-made ocean fissures.
Watching seasons of sunsets pass, I think
of those pale, unrealized creatures
and of him
recumbent in a field of asphodel
waiting....

SCARLETT

...Tara

Look — I'm not flying. This is levitation
in a fetal position, hovering below
the blanched ceiling, hands on my head.

At first it seems to be the mansion dream —
burnished walnut panels,
circular stairs with galleries where
you grasp my shoulder calling the house
a godsend, not paralyzing
nightmare. But this space is alabaster;
and I linger buoyed in vapor, while
Bonnie and a ring of pinafored children
applaud, their timpani voices mingled with
plummy scent of their bodies.
I hear the sibilant in and out sigh
of my own breath. Breathe, pant,
skim, push, expel; yet never dismiss

the power that free-floats me where
nothing can touch, nothing but
fragrance and echoes of infant laughter.

LENA GROVE

...Yoknapatawpha County

"Pickup, pick up them broken pieces
and take them to the Lord.... "

Shadowdappled womanflesh —
something moving forever and without
progress across an urn.

Under a jonquilcolored sun,
in too-big man's shoes, she walks,
placid, face smooth
as a stone yet not hard. Appreciative
because people can be kind,

she chooses to be surprised by passion,
fecundity, sweetsuckling
of a brier-patch child.
She may be *a forgotten bead*
from a broken string; but dreaming

moongleamed shapes, she — aware
of train whistles at a crossing miles away —
carries on.

"Pickup, pick up them broken pieces
and take them to the Lord.... "

BLANCHE

... Royal Orleans

Often I'm unsure which door is
mine or which floor. Purseless,
unpocketed, I cringe as
flocked wallpaper stencils my arms.
Must I retreat, wheedle
keys for a room that belongs
to a name I can't recall?

Am I wearing shoes? Will this
elevator stop? Shall I angle left?
Right? Do my palms exude chlorine?
Is last week's polish mooned
beneath my nail? Then with conjured
magic I'm poised by a door,
willing it to yield. It opens.

Queasy, I see Redon blossoms,
Rousseau beasts, Dali timepieces;
and I relish empowerment
as silent hinges pivot me. But why
surreal rooms? Why not chasms
without trestles, seas without
ships, the rim of a volcano?

Impossible.
Keyed-up, and my feet are bare.

WHAT MARGARET KNEW

...Howards End

Circumvent was what Margaret knew best.
Smile when you ache to bite or scratch.
The life of the mind is superior yet not all.
He came as a grain of sand beneath her skin.
Draped in sackcloth, he courted.
She, clear-eyed, nodded. *My love-making,*
she told her sister softly, *will be prose.*

Calm, she overlooked obtuseness: the way
he bore their wedding as a funeral. Later,
inhaling a river of hyacinth and narcissus,
she fixed her gaze on the wych-elm,
aware, as she wiped husks from lanterns,
of unrealized nymphs who once sought light.
Comforts are of two kinds, said Margaret,

who kept herself in hand, *those we can share*
with others, like fire, weather, or music;
and those we can't — food, for instance.
Then, at midnight, chin on counterpane,
she tasted pearls, aware she'd earned
them, each lustrous one. *Good-bye, good-bye,*
good-bye, she breathed. *Ebb of a dying sea.*

YELENA'S KISS

...Estate Serebriakoff

Autumn roses — charming sad roses
infected with my idleness...
Fingers steepled, she paces, talking
to herself, numbering stones beneath
her feet. When she was young,
she echoed the roses' peachy essence,
inhaled it with a child's exuberance.
Then scale and thorn
infected all. Now, old, she halts
beside the bushes recalling

blossoms grown fat in
the sun, badgers hunted by owl-light
in sacheted air. Shivering, she
snaps off a full-formed bud
to keep for her sweet-wood chest.
Soon, like Vanya, she'll sit indoors
gazing outward. *Linden tea,* she muses,
pressing the bud's damp lips against
hers, tonguing them, savoring
one last kiss, *or maybe raspberry.*

ANNA

...Moscow

Above our bed, an invisible mesh
of hairnet seines brittle-gray curls.
A head without a body bobs
as hands with no arms ripple air.

That face looms, and insomnia sucks
like a slick freshwater eel. Afraid,
I cry, "Who are you? What do you want?"
Then with my nails, I rake at flesh

until eyes float the night — eyes hazed
by a film of years; and, at last, I know
that woman.
She sees why I can't dream. Gazing

at me angled by your body, she feels
my restlessness, my pain; and, neither
curious nor gloating, she says,
"I remember loving. I remember love."

MOLLY HAS THE LAST WORD

...7 Eccles Street

Yes love lovers frigging sex the smell of a man
thats all anyone ever supposes I think about
dresses perfume flesh roses men getting up under
my petticoats and giving kisses
long and hot down to my soul and forget that like
other women I am sensitive can cry
yet you see I know more than most because of the word
because I read and have not only a soul but
gray matter too like the men
o rocks I dont know metempsychosis still with Calypso
barelolling above my brass bed I know winedark seas
have my own copy of Lord Byrons poems
as well as three pairs of gloves
lying here Ive read Wilkie Collins Moonstone
Rabelais East Lynne almost any book as long as it
hasnt a Molly in it
and bytheby have a passing acquaintance with Jane
Emma Tess Anna and some of their sisters
even if theyre all afraid to say what I say except
maybe Dame Alys of Bath for she like me is
yes earthy honest and somewhat taken with a bit of lace
a nice sort of brooch or young loins
and would know how to act when a man wanted to
milk her sweet and thick into his tea
but come from another time she hasnt had to listen to
bumgut filthyminded Dr Freud seen him kick up
a row trying to find out what it is women want
though he never asked me
yes of course I could have told him yes
for with my life and reading and knowing

women are sisters under their skins
this answers simple like the nose on his face and it is
power yes power we want
then people would be a fat lot better
and youd never see this much killing or drunkenness
so power it is in love in sex in war and you can
go all the way back if you wish to the ancient Greeks
to those sisters Fates Muses Seaside girls and the rest
yes they knew what they wanted as I know what I want
power but particularly the power
men have been least willing to give us
still with an Andalusian rose in my hair I will possess it
yes the power of the word
yes thats what women want yes the word yes

Bright And Dusky Tones

THE MAN WHO STOOD ON A CHAIR

In 1929, my father hung up his skates,
red-penciled one last *Daily Cardinal,* then
leased himself to the family realty business.
Given the year, writing
the great American novel was not an option.
So closing that door, making way for
Bellow and Malamud, my father rented studios,
subletting the Olive Street store to Sol Jacobs
who sold suits with two pairs of trousers.

By the time I began to imprint memory,
my father was a job-curdled man
who escaped each night to the arms of
a La-Z-Boy where, as images blurred on TV,
he thumbed through *Life.* Inflated from
skating-trim to a mid-life 190, chewing gum,
lamenting steering wheel shimmy
in his Olds 88 or his bogie on the dog-leg 17th,
he exuded a Babbitt-y aura.

Then last fall in Santa Monica, 13 years after
his death, I crashed a party
and met a man from Missouri who told me
of the night my father stood on a chair.
At a banquet in a ballroom where
each person was asked to say his name,
a child, someone's granddaughter,
had stood on a chair to introduce herself.
Then my father, chuckling, had done the same.

That night in my hotel, I stared in the mirror,
pondering this clue. Later, unable
to unearth either sleep or the phantom
who had been my father, I chased down corridors,
searching. Toward morning, maddened by
half-cracked doors, I keened, aware
I would never catch the man —
novelist *manqué*, streak of the Silver Skates,
who wrote STET on galleys or had the spontaneity
to confront 300 people standing on a chair.

THE SOUND OF YOUR MOTHER CHEWING

Sometime in childhood you begin to hear it,
know her teeth are starting to chip,
discolor as fillings
and crowns pulp food. Her swallows
are intolerable, intake of breath,
the touch of her hand.
Still, shrinking from toothmarks
or fingerprints, you
consider texture and taste, covet them.

Grasshopper, caterpillar, cricket chew
and keep chewing.
Children keep them in jars,
listen at night before all chewing grates
and touch hints of mortality.
Children, though alert to decay,
choose to pretend
their glass-walled caterpillars are
not chewing patiently toward oblivion.

Across great distances, countless mouths
chew. Mother's, too,
as she reaches and strains
to touch me again. *Tell me*, I call into
space, *what you know about
flavor and rapture.* Her mouth opens,
but instead of sound, butterflies arc.
Instead of ordinary touch,
I feel a dusting of pollen on my hand.

MINIMALISM

Chicago, my mother, sister, and I
were taking one last trip:
the Art Institute to see my cousin's show.
Tom, a mimimalist — only 30 and
already a star — sculpts with string,
pencil-shavings, aspirin, bubble gum,
mucus, soap, pubic hair.

Tulips, daffodils, and pear trees were
blooming outside, and inside
hotel walls were rampant with roses.
At night, my sister and I sprawled on
flowered beds like young girls as
Mother sat on a loveseat in a purple gown
flaking skin from her legs. They
were swollen, studded with keloids,
and I stared at them as her voice
graveled on reliving dinner, the art show,
other dinners and shows and clothing,

other wallpapers remembered from
long-vanished rooms. She sat talking
until the carpet at her feet
was white with a thousand petals
of dead skin. *Look,* she said, as she
rose to pick her way to her room,
I've snowed all over your floor....

When morning came and I paused
by the loveseat to tie my shoes,

my sister cringed and told me
I was standing on
Mother's body. As I side-stepped
toward the window, gazed out
at pear blossoms clouding a fierce
spring wind, my sister covered
our mother with Sunday funnies
and said we'd better not call Tom.

FUGITIVES

The foam Pratone chair from '66 is brittle
like toothpicks. Nesting bowls of '46 — a toxic blob.
Old fill in the Saarinen womb has turned to sand,
and Mother's wedding dress
hangs in my closet willfully raveling.

Some everyday materials — those used in clothing
and design: plastics, fibers, papers — are fugitive,
unstable and prone to reactions that can't be
stemmed. But degradation isn't new. Ancient bronzes
oxidize, and 17th century glass weeps.

Easy come, easy go, my father used to say before
he turned fugitive and fled. Now Mother, sloughing
cartons of letters, brown-edged pictures
of those lovers I never knew, embraces
transience, prepares to leave me and sleuth after him.

As western canyons erode and blue glaciers dwindle,
as poppies riot the meadows then shrivel
in August sun, our parents, our past, our rare things
will one by one turn fugitive. So forget conservation.
Let the distressed fail as they will.

PALATINO

Feeling well-defended, I tender him the poem
about our father, the one about the night he
stood on a chair. My brother, showing

unexpected emotion, bends to my words, calls
his wife, *Here, look.* I — pleased to have
moved him — dish up curry while they confer.

At last, my brother says, *Listen, we need
to know. This type-face. What is it?
Perfect, don't you think, for annual reports?*

As he speaks, saffron fogs my eyes. Saffron,
vegetable gold, most precious of spices,

culled from purpled *crocus sativus* picked as
it opens and pollen-harvested by hand.
One hundred thousand flowers yield but

a pound of seasoning. So what is precious?
A spice, the image of a dead father who once
greeted three hundred people standing on a chair?

I've never shown work to my brother, never
before tried to disarm him. Now eyeing him
from afar, I stand alone in a field of

crocus sativus. *Palatino,* I tell him. Then, soon,
I change all my words from Palatino to Times.

QUIZ KID

According to her mother, she read
Grimm and the phone book
before she was two.
By the time she was nine, she knew
Eleanor Roosevelt, Maurice Evans,
Judy Garland and had been on the radio
140 times. There she answered
questions, especially ones about
William Shakespeare. Yes,
she's the girl in
that photograph, perched
(in jumper and white eyelet blouse)
on a nest of fan mail.
See how docilely her knees cross, how
patent leather shoes mirror
flocks of letters to which her mother,
signing her name, penned replies.
But wait, there's more. When she was
thirteen, she combed out those pigtails,
published *Caliban's Surprise*.
And by the time she reached twenty,
she was a wife, a parent,
a Phi Beta Kappa. Since then,
she's rummaged through years,
quizzing herself. *Who am I?*
When was the last time someone wrote?
Why do I always feel as if I'm
making an exit pursued by a bear?

BALANCHINE BALLERINA

We were on a bare stage somewhere,
hot under blue gels, and Balanchine wanted
to make sure I was strong.

Instead of admitting ankle-sprain,
I retied ribbons on my practice shoes
and stretched hamstrings at the barre.

Balanchine told me to do a *plié;* then
pressing his hand in the small of my back,
another. *No arch*, he said, *flatten it.*

Not nineteen or any linear age,
I could feel skin-color tights webbing at
the crotch, pleating below the knee

as I remembered how he loathed im-
perfection. Reaching to smooth my tights,
he touched my thigh, said, *You're*

getting fat. Silent, I turned from the barre,
stuck a pin in him once, then again until
he began to shrivel, until he popped.

Limping past pools of hot blue light,
I found a girl-child hunkered
in the wings, arranging animals from

Noah's Ark. She was hanging them
from a broomstick two by two, suspending
each pair by their necks with silver wire.

A frayed tutu jutted below her belly,
and her laddered tights sagged at the knee.
Looking up, she arched her back

and picking a scab from her elbow
asked why I had popped my balloon.

MORNING TRANSMOGRIFICATION

Water needles her head, shoulders;
and the scent of fresh-cracked coconut,
seeping after windfall, bathes
her cheeks. In this damp-hot
tropic shower, her body diminishes.
Length and slope dwindle, body hair recedes,
restoring her to nymph.

The coconut, her shampoo promises,
is emulsified with chamomile,
aloe, honey, rosemary, citron, nettles.
Somehow, purveyors of soap have intuited
all: essence of age twelve,
shrink-wrapped for morning
transmogrifications

                    to pre-pubescent innocence.
Caressing her slick-sapling flanks,
aroused by awareness of an unbudded form
never before revered, she tastes droplets
spilling from her head
and remembers
not the coconut but the nettles.

Season Of Burnt Offerings

Maple singes the ridges and sumac the hillside
in this season of burnt offerings.
                    October light
where morning pools under flamed trees
and a plane hawks the sky.

On the Assabet, leaf boats eddy when canoe
knifes water. I can and do stroke like this
in my sleep, the paddle
                    an extension of my arms,
heart and breath aligned
while turtles sun atop boulders
                    and a young heron
poises on one leg in the brush.

                    Last fall among mangroves,
shark and manta below, sea turtles coupled,
we approached another heron
near Fernandina as I,
                    with imprinted strength
angled the Zodiac like an Old Town canoe,

surprised to be curved again inside the girl
who paddled, portaged, faced thunder
or rapids unblinking
                    before it was autumn
where sinus-ache predicts snow
and memory saps strength.

Once a storm-chaser, now a sleep-traveler
stroking time, remembering how blue

seared the water's skin

> with a deeper heat,

remembering burnt-out ends of kisses,
burnt leaves of love.

Sun is arcing low behind ridges;

> arms and chest ache

as darkness drinks up sunlight
and I turn, struggle upstream seeing not heron
hidden in the brush

> but sun-brown girl

shy, poised, denying winter
and ripe to dream of summer's heat.

FALSE PREGNANCY

Uneasy morning sleep
spilled skeins of spring-tinged yarn.
As that wool tumbled,
I fondled it, informing
some sheepish shopkeeper of the sacque
I would knit. Already I could feel
strands purl
like moss, glimpse an infant
blinking with blind seer's eyes.

At home,
I'd have been at Jana's place
on Sacramento Street,
buying a cable hook and oiled Aran
to make myself a hooded coat of
off-white diamonds; but instead,
I could sense my belly swell, my navel
distend one more time.

Oh, babies who loom at dawn, you milk
me with your gaze. Who
are you? What do you require?
And where can I discover
how to block or true
the old ones?

FLOSSIE

When I peered through the mail slot, I saw
her on the walk, black face set, turning
toward the street. Martha and the others
lingered, convinced I'd materialize,
smile, greet Flossie and her church-sisters.

A daytime nap had conjured them; but, called
by a Person from Porlock, I woke to the grating
din of a political pitch. I hung up. Then,
more resolute than Coleridge, I burrowed back.

Martha stepped in first. *Looking fine,* I said,
aware she was arrayed for choir practice,
not for cleaning houses. Above caftan and
braids, she'd angled a veiled hat. I hugged
her, and she fanned Passion toward my nostrils.
Skinny thang, she said, *not fat and nice
and greasy like us. Not yet old as white thread.*

Playing hostess, I collected shawls, purses,
primed the kettle but at the same time
watched Flossie who was inexplicably clothed
in my new red-flowered silk. She was mute.

What? I whispered, aware of years tolled since
the funeral I had not managed to attend. *What?*

Spoons rattled. I poured, apologized for sweets
by Nabisco and because the quince snowed petals.
Still, Flossie in my silk, not one I'd given

her, did not speak. Finally as I shivered
tea leaves in the hollow of my cup,
she touched me. *Baby... Baby...* she said.

Why are you here? I asked. *Why did you leave?*
Since then, no one has taken care of me right.

Flossie, daubed her neck with a kerchief.
She nodded. Then, sloe-eyed, she beckoned.
Baby... she said, beginning to unbutton
the front of the dress that belonged to me. *Baby....*

FLESH

When I pinch it, a ridge of faded peach faille
slowly flattens out.
Once, it resembled skin of the sleeping newborn
crooked in my elbow: satiny,
sensuous to the touch.
Today, scarred, pocked and stenciled, it forms
porous, rippled plains. Just when I came to enjoy
it, modeled like a sleek self-shawl, it began
to stretch, creping topographical maps
along neck and arms.
Now veins river them, river my legs, too.
Shirred rosettes dot my hands; and when I fist
them, knobs of bone project.
That bone with its pallor suggests
the whited bone and sack of skin which,
long before death, was my husband's mother.
Lift her and she caved in as though,
over time, she'd forgotten her imprint.

But I recall mine; so when the baby, my grandson,
awakens, I — stirred by archaic impulses —
unbutton, unhook, and respond.
Cupping my teat, I edge it toward his mouth.
As he latches on, the half-remembered
pull and clamp unnerve me.
Oblivious to my agitation, the child burrows
into damp flesh.
Then he arches, rears his head,
outraged he has been tendered a sham:
no firmness, no lushness, no milk.
I, similarly outraged, match him howl for howl.

WASHRAG

Something has happened.
Whereas once my speech sluiced
like water over a spillway,
smooth and satisfying,
now it often gaps, presents
moments where, as silence wrings
my tongue, no word appears. A few grains
of sand scatter through the glass;
and words riffle to the surface, leaking,
overlapping, repeating, dribbling
transposed syllables, confused consonants.

Oh, please help, my mother-in-law
once pleaded. *Something is happening
to me.* But I, still facile then frowned,
as I scrawled her signature
on the nursing home forms, while she
whispered that some person
with a washrag was scrubbing her brain away.
Now years later, I feel as if she
is plying her washrag inside my head.

MOURNING CLOAK

Her voice was hushed when she told me
of the mourning cloak:
yellow and black inlaid with blue.
She'd found it floating on the surface
of her pool, and — despite her fear of
dead things — had lifted it
from crazed water, laid it in the grass,
then turned to clip her roses.
Only a moment later, she insists,
the butterfly was gone, resurrected
into a spring day. Exhilarated,
the woman described the miracle,
how she'd saved a speck of beauty, preserving
life as pollen grains sheened the margins
of her nails. This is her story.

Had it been mine, I'd have mingled awe
with skepticism, invoked wedges of
parallel time and lifted my dead-seeming child
from pools in which she sought to drown.
I'd have let myself be sucked back
to when she — frail and lovely
as the butterfly — dressed herself as
Ophelia, pale cheek, pale dress,
dark shawl flecked with blue and took
the fork which drew her to the left.
This time, I'd hold her hand and we'd
wade right together. Then I'd lift
her from the water, spread her wings,
lay her on grass so she
could warm and fly whole into morning.

But I'm a cynic, and it's not my story.
Through scrims of light, I see no resurrection,
feel dead means dead. A drowned butterfly
cannot reclaim life, so I see a simpler explanation:
a red-wing blackbird who alit
to beak and swallow
a mourning cloak as a woman sheared roses.

SPIDER

Embers of the fire flare, exhale heat.
Staring, she contemplates webs
of gray-white blurring the log.

Overlaid, her eyes see things
that can't be real. Her grown child
white and thin holding a baby

against the wind. Fire settles, blanches.
Crack of wood consumed by flame is
like crack of dry grass underfoot

by the riverbed and vineyard where
last grapes raisin on the vine.
They are walking, and the mother stops,

shows the sacred datura, its dark
prickled leaves, white blossom,
thorny seed pod. As always,

even a late-season plant is
a lesson: nightshade or jimson,
locoweed, too: poisonous,

hallucinogenic. The daughter
shifts the baby from hip to hip, nods
looking yet not looking. A spider

cakewalks from the shadowed flower,
an albino, ethereal, lovely,
white as angelfood,

white as disbelief. The daughter averts
her head, eases the baby to
her breast, and spindles slowly away.

The mother stares at frail legs.
Her eyes close. What she sees
is pale as cooling ashes, pale as bone.

BONES

They are beautiful, she tells him. Elemental,
stripped down, pure. He'd just watched her
crawl from an Incan rock tomb
where she'd dug up
a single gray-white knuckle,
to tuck in the pack that holds beak and
legbone of an albatross.

At home, she has sea lion scapulae
from Baja, ribs of deer and boar,
camel vertebrae from Petra.
She tells him of immigration in Amman
when she was held until agents
found them in her bag and,
laughing maniacally, waved her through.

She describes watching bones roil
in the La Brea Tar Pits,
of seeing them entombed in blue-white
glacial ice, of how — after the accident —
she touched the uncanny whiteness
of her son's skull.

First, as storyteller, she relates these things.
Then looking away, she says,
They are props for my ghost dance.
They exorcise images of
our flesh deserting our bones.

WINTER SOLSTICE

1. Baba

In the cellar, on a rusted lawn chair
beside the water heater, I find
our Baba. Wearing black lace-ups
with cubed heels, a dress with
handsewn buttonholes — identical except
where her waist makes one grin,
she stares at me until hectic spots stain
cheeks. Light penetrates high,
fly-specked windows and illuminates
hairnet spider-webbing
her forehead below folds of

pale sheitel. Around her: detritus
of decades. Our cellar is for things
which have no use. First we stockpile
them at the stairs. Then by the door.
At last, below, they molder on shelves
or atop the child-sized workbench:
a drum, old Lincoln Logs, last year's
canceled checks. Eyes passing over
all, aware of heat and drip of
water heater, I stare again at Baba.
What are you doing in the cellar? I ask.

Rolling socks, she tells me. *Like most
bubbes I stay at home and roll socks.*
Now her cheeks deepen. *Or sometimes,
at night, I roll in sweet-scented hay...*

> *But Baba, it's dark and damp,*
I tell her. *You don't belong down here.*
She smiles, layers one thick-fingered hand
over the other. *Oh, I do, my Dumpling,*
she replies slowly, *because upstairs*
in your fine house, I forget to
roll and can't ever remember my name.

2. Mother

Poised before her scale, Mother — arbiter
of family myths — weighs truth against
fabrication. *It never happened,*
she insists, balancing her perceptions,
discarding mine. *Baba*
was Grampa Jack's mother's mother,
dead before you were born.

> *Still,* I insist, *she was*
there, sitting in the dark dressed in
worsted. With hands shaped like mine,
and a long face. She spoke to me.

Mother, unwilling to pardon unreality,
adjusts her blindfold, recalibrates,
scoffs at me. *Then it's*
her photograph you remember.
Just a picture. We used to store it in
the cellar wedged between
our furnace and the hot water heater.

3. Self

Shuffle, step, shuffle, step. Down in
the cellar I am tapping out all the bright
things that Mother and everyone tell me
are not true. *Shuffle, scuff, turn.*
Look at me. Then look again.
My cane, my hat — both are props,
for I am not yet Baba, not yet my mother.
Still, upstairs, I can't practice on
satin-finish floors, because I'll scar them.
So, between furnace and water heater,
using the workbench as barre,
I dance.

I dance against time, against rage. Days
are short now.

                    Baba danced in Szumsk,
I'm sure, but never here. Looking on,
she finds me as disconcerting as my house:
strong-hipped, grown woman in black
skivvies, socks, and TeleTones tapping
into gathering darkness. *Why?* she asks.
Because, I answer, eyeing squared hands.
Shuffle, flap. Shuffle-hop, toe.
Because as winter comes, I, too, need
time — *shuffle, roll* — to contemplate
sweet-scented hay.

FORGIVENESS

Sometimes, I buy old quilts but never ones
with any stain. No tea, no blood,
or fluids that will not succumb to Tide.
This work, tendered by a woman from
Missouri, is Ocean Waves, 1890 — white
with hand-dipped blue — loved, necessary.

Its pattern is, at once, exuberant, contained,
a triangulated flow of motion.
Yearning, I stretch my hands; yet when we
(the woman from Missouri and I) sail
the quilt outside on her line, there,
borne on the crest of a wave, is a mark.
India ink. An exclamation point. Indelible.

The ink, I'm sure (men do not write in bed),
was dropped by a woman. Rorschached,
I stare until I see someone
who dreamed oceans and words.
I know how, propped on pillows, fingers
callused from milking, stitch-pitted,
she scrawled. Alone at night, she stole
time to piece thoughts. But the quilt has

a stain. "No," I tell the woman from
Missouri. Still, that quilter, glances up
from her tablet, squints across time, summons
me, alien of the future. I do not move.
Irked by my caution, she gestures
with her pen. A drop falls, leaving
a message that will last a hundred years.

"Stained," I murmur, undulated by
Ocean Waves, glancing toward the woman
from Missouri. She's speaking, but her words
lap past as I (asking if anything of mine
will last a hundred years) hear only
the other one, the one with the pen.
Head, hand, heart, she urges. *Courage.*
Eyes salted, I nod. Then, for what we cannot
change, I forgive us both.

SWIMMERS

Exultation is the going
Of an inland soul to sea...
— Emily Dickinson

Cirrus fishtails above peaks, and arcs
of silver bream the water while I
drift from shore. Bobbing alone,
I glide until stalled by shoal of rock.

As I push off, rock gives, humps
over then under waves,
because it is not rock but sea turtle
finning through sheened water.

Sculling backwards, I find another,
then another. Around me
black-green chelonia — a phalanx of
armored presences — swim.

Soon we are stroking forth, pitch
and yaw as one. Should we
incline toward shore? How long will
strength buoy us and grant breath?

Even as questions float, I cease to care.
Gold and ruby eyes see for me.
Toothless mid-Triassic mouths speak
for me. Together, we are charmed,

so as sunset bleeds across skin
of water, anxiety ebbs; and I,
choired by manatee, feel
swells of communion and of grace.

MERMAIDS

They dive and fluke their way down
where coral burgeons
and a moray eel jabs his head
toward caverns that phosphoresce
blinking crevices to unreality.
And water undulates
without intent until its currents
draw them through stippled tunnels, mazes
where angelfish and Moorish idol nudge them
as they plunge, swerve, tangled ribbons of hair fanning,
never pausing, pulling, thrusting,
a mystery of the unrehearsed,
their scales: stars in pooled darkness
dimming as they descend,
their hands seining water,
breasts canting outward as they stroke
exhaling bubbled strands,
singing to dolphin and humpback.
Oh, don't forget us,
best beloveds, for we can still breathe songs
and, though sheathed, can love
with eyes, hands, lips, tongues, for
freedom and betrayal are in the mind,
and we may be myths men fashioned,
but the eel will snap his jaw,
acknowledge our sway.
His force knows force and makes no other claims,
aware we've left our abalone mirrors and combs
within reach of the rising tide.

LIVING IN CURVED SPACE

She inhales stars until she is light-filled
and can bat-wing above the dark earth.

Another out-of-body sequence and
her flanks fur, throat chuffs, tail grows.

As a fish shifts color when it fins from light
into shadow or a chameleon on a twig, she

stretches herself on a Persian carpet until
she absorbs its bright and dusky tones,

its curlicues, swags, and feathered wreaths
and is invisible to those who come for her.

Below the high dam, the real Abu-Simbil lies.
Below the sea, the lighthouse of Pharos.

There are worlds, too — under lava, under ice —
where no tree falls and no sound is heard.

What is hidden will not again be visible. She
seeks refuge in these places: angles of repose

where salmon turn to seagulls and a hand
may, to infinity, hold a pen and draw itself.

I am walking down a tunnel, lantern
angled aloft. Behind fused lids I see sparklers,
Roman candles streaking red-orange on walls,
and I hear echoes of a thousand voices.
Don't hold me accountable for the truth
because it has a wide spectrum. Still, listen.
Don't go away. In this place, fact and fiction
roil with time and space while I surge
forward. Beneath my feet, sand undulates,
sifting random hints in cuffs, between toes.
Here, pinks of Hakone's cherries fuse
with flesh-tint of infants I have cradled.
But behind sweetness of blossom and babe,
I detect odor of prey, of other people's tears.

When I reach out, the wall roughs the ends
of yellowed fingertips, and I see with them.
At this moment, I know Machu Picchu, Masada,
Black Hills of Dakota — places I've never been.
Objective details matter less than ones
that flick shadows upon a scrim. Straining,
I find peacocks, an iceberg, Tower of Babel;
yet all are evolving shapes of my hand.
I know illusion but cannot joust with anything
except a specter of reality. I am asleep in
a waking dream. Don't block my path or
rouse me. I must keep walking. The journey
is more than its story. Truth is beyond touch;
and water in the tunnel is lapping feet.

Flotsam and jetsam drag at ankles,
lurch toward knees. Seaweed fingers probe
until I want to cry for mercy.
Instead, eyes still closed, I wade through water
while mustard-green kelp burbles past.
Underfoot, popping and pull of tide,
salt-scent of sea, of blood. This intimidates,
and I give in. Because my arm is heavy,
I give in. I have no lantern. I never had one.
It was Diogenes. Or Dante pacing Circles of Hell.
As the tunnel twists, I wonder if
I'm the one on every water journey who springs
from the high rock, and if so then what?
If I turn back, I'll never speak in tongues.

Exactitude wavers as water, shading blue,
rises buoying me. Eddies suck layers
of time. In this place, time stagnates
and tide is process. I opt for process.
Swimming now, hands cupped as my father
showed me, aware of his voice,
an indigo whisper, *Another country heard from.*
Hope springs eternal. Oddly, the tunnel's
spectrum is unspecified — light turns
red to green, and green purples. More water
flows. Either I am gilled, breathing
silkily, or I'm skimming between wave
and tunnel arch, inhaling violet ether,
singing as a golden ray beckons.

Comforted by hints of warmth, I pull
myself from waters, nest in colorless linen
with a thicket of arms, legs not all my own.
Jangled, I cannot rest; so I reimmerse
in scudding currents. Fact and fiction purl
murmuring: *Do not try to hold me.*
I will evade. I will lie.
Listening, I open my hands, my lids.
Though colors overlapped should be black,
here they are gold; and instead of water, I see
an unblinking eye, find myself in curved space
where the eye, aware I'm consumed
by shadow matter, does not exact blame
as its gold spirals sparks to tinder me.